OPEN HERAT

The Transforming Power of God's Love

By: Heidy Mejia

Table of Content

HEIDY MEJÍA

Other Books written by
Heidy Mejía in English and Spanish

1. Beyond my Wounds
2. The Power of Forgiveness

Spanish:
3. Mas Alla de Mis Heridas
4. El Poder del Perdón

Books written in English and Spanish by Tony
Mejía (Heidy Mejía) Husband

English:
1. From The Streets to The Altar
2. A Journey to Redemption
3. Morning Blessings & Mercies

Spanish:
1. De Las Calles al Altar
2. El Camino A la Redención
3. Bendiciones y Misericordias de la Mañana

Introduction

I invite you to engage yourself in a unique experience in the pages of this book, where emotions flow freely, and divine love becomes the reason for a profound transformation. "Open Heart" is more than a title; it is a call to discover the true meaning of life through the transforming power of God's love.

In life, every human being is marked with both good and bad experiences.

The bad ones are inevitable and many times we remember them or hold on to them, so we live full of fears and limitations among other things.

In the word of God, we can find tools that will help us overcome any obstacle or situation. In the Bible there are many stories where in each of them we can see how the Power and Love of God we can overcome, and our end will be a glorious one of which we can testify and help others.

This book not only tells stories; it takes you through an experience that transcends words. Explore how God's love can overcome obstacles, heal wounds, and change lives. "Open Heart" is a window to the divine power that is at the center of our being. Every page of this book is filled with the essence of divine love, from moving stories to deep reflections. This book not only aims to amuse us, but also to inspire and guide us, reminding us that God's love is always present in our lives.

I invite you to read all the way till the end and allow the transformative power of God's divine love to envelop you. Learn how every word, every story, reminds us of the infinite goodness that surrounds us. Are you ready to participate in a journey of self-knowledge, healing, and renewal through the transformative power of love?

Therefore, I'm waiting for you with open arms!

Chapter 1

A story that emphasizes the value of free will and the consequences of our decisions is the biblical account of Cain and Abel. Although Cain and Abel were the sons of Adam and Eve, their free will choices led to significant changes in their lives.

Abel dedicated himself to the care of the flocks as a shepherd, while Cain cultivated the land and took care of the crops. Both decided to offer God a part of their products at any given time. Abel presented the best of his flock, including the portions of fat, while Cain offered an offering of fruits and vegetables. It is important to note that God gave Cain and Abel total freedom to decide what to offer, without imposing any rules on them.

God gladly accepted Abel's offering but rejected Cain's. This caused in Cain an intense pain for his brother's rejection, thus feeding feelings of resentment, jealousy, and anger. In his infinite wisdom, God spoke to Cain to confront what was happening in his heart. "Why are you angry?" He asked. "Why do you have that expression of sadness? If you follow the right path, won't you be accepted? However, sin is stalking your door, wanting to dominate you. You must control it."

Cain ended up killing his brother. Through the story of Cain and Abel, we learn important things and we can see how his heart's intentions were exposed to adversity.

This story teaches us how we should be careful with the feelings, emotions and desires of the flesh that are contrary to the fruit of the Holy Spirit. Cain was envious of his brother because God gladly accepted Abel's offering.

We can say that God already knew Cain's heart and, in a way, was giving him an opportunity for Cain to see what he kept in his heart (Adversity exposes what you have inside) and God wanted to give him the opportunity to make the right decision and overcome any contrary feeling, such as envy, so that he could form his character. The decision was in the hands of Cain, Genesis 4:7 says: "If you do good, won't you be accepted? But if you don't do it well, sin lurks at the door; his desire is to have power over you, but you must dominate it." 8 And Cain said to his brother, "Let's go out into the field." And once in the field, he killed him.

In the same way, God gives us the freedom to choose between doing good or evil, choosing to bear fruit even in adversity or being dragged by sinful nature.

Acting under impulses or emotions brings serious consequences to our lives and those around us. We can even say hurtful words under an impulse or in a moment of pressure or frustration, causing deep wounds, and then regret it, but maybe it's too late. We must learn to be responsible for our emotions, attitudes, and decisions we make. We have no excuses or sufficiently justified reasons to act with evil without considering the consequences or harming others.

When God tried to confront Cain for the worst crime committed, he evaded his responsibility, but before God there was no justifiable excuse and he accepted them. This teaches us that we must take responsibility for our actions and be honest.

We must take advantage of adversity to reflect on what we keep in our hearts and ask God to cleanse us of all evil. The ability to choose between good and evil is a crucial component of free will, as revealed in God's words to Cain. God gave Cain the opportunity to choose the right course of action, overcome his bad feelings and follow the path of justice. He reminded Cain that, in the end, he was responsible for his own actions and warned him about the pernicious influence of sin.

Unfortunately, Cain ignored God's advice and called his brother Abel to the field, where he killed him driven by envy. This violent act revealed Cain's inability to take advantage of his free will in a positive way. He allowed bitterness and anger to consume him, which had inevitable consequences.

God did not prevent Cain from electing to assassinate his brother, but he did confront Cain after the fact. "Where is your brother Abel?" He asked. Feeling the weight of shame and guilt, Cain replied: "Am I my brother's guardian?", to avoid taking responsibility (Genesis 4:9). As a just punishment from God, Cain was banished from his family and from the land he cultivated.

The story of Abel and Cain offers a powerful lesson about free will and the value of making moral decisions. Cain was given the opportunity to show his devotion and faith in God by choosing how to present his offering. However, Cain's choice to allow his bad feelings to control him had disastrous results.

This narrative also demonstrates the limitations of free will. God warned Cain about the repercussions of his actions, but in the end, it was Cain who had to exercise moderation and make the right decision. God showed his respect for our ability to make decisions in this way, even when those decisions have unfavorable effects.

The story of Cain and Abel serves as a useful reminder that, although we have been granted free will as a gift, we also have a responsibility to use it responsibly. We have the power to make decisions that glorify God, promote compassion, and love, and generate good things. However, we must also be aware of the possible repercussions of our actions and strive to make morally correct and fair decisions.

Chapter 2

Let Yourself be Molded

Adversity, trials, difficulties, diseases, scarcity, the loss of a loved one and any situation that seems opposite can be used as a platform, as an opportunity to examine ourselves and work in areas of our lives such as anxiety, health, and forgiveness.

Romans 8:28 tells us that we know that God works in every situation for the good of those who love him.

God has given us the ability to differentiate between the good and the bad, not to point out to others, but to see ourselves through the Bible and allow God and his Holy Spirit to form us. In this way, we can give pleasant fruits that others will see and want to enjoy, being also transformed. The word of God says, "By their fruits you will know them." And to bear good fruit, we must have a healthy heart.

Psalm 119:105 tells us that the Word of God is a lamp at our feet and a lamp on our way. In the Word of God, we will find what we need to overcome.

When God allows a situation in your life, even if it seems otherwise, remember that everything God allows is for the purpose of forming us, healing us, and strengthening our faith in Him.

On one occasion, I was going to cook farina (oatmeal) and for that I needed milk. The first thing I did was go get the gallon of milk and make sure that the expiration date was not overdue. I smelled it and everything seemed to indicate that it was in good condition to be used. However, when putting it on the fire, the milk was damaged, its texture and smell changed. The more it got hot, the more evident it was that it was damaged, so I couldn't use it, since it would hurt me to consume it, as well as my family.

At that moment, the Spirit of God ministries in my life and told me: "This is how it often happens in people's lives. On the outside they seem to be good, healthy, and even attractive, but when the difficulty comes, adversity exposes what is in their heart. I allow this for the human being to sit and reflect on their attitudes, their character, their way of speaking and treating others in situations such as frustration, deception, loss, pain, illness, fear, etc. It is the perfect opportunity for us to accept that there are areas in our lives that need to be molded and transformed through the power and love of God."

I invite you to reflect and ask God to show you the areas you need to strengthen, especially in difficult times.

Questions you can ask yourself.

1. How do I react when someone offended me?

____

____

____

____

2. What is my response to a character that has offended me?

____

____

____

____

3. When I pray, I ask for mercy for those who offended and hurt me? Or do I ask for revenge?

____

____

____

____

Write your answer and ask the Holy Spirit to guide you and help strengthen these areas, so that even in times of adversity you can glorify God with your life and actions, and others can recognize that you are a child of God. This way you can bear pleasant fruits and be a living testimony of the faith you have in Him.

Chapter 3

Esther is an incredible story of courage, faith, and disinterest. It tells the story of a young Jewish woman named Esther who, in an act of courage and determination, put her own life in danger to avoid the annihilation of the Jewish people. This moving story reminds us of the importance of defending what is right, even when doing so puts us in danger.

Esther, a beautiful woman, lost her parents when she was very young and was raised by her uncle Mordecai. At that time, there was a king named Ahasuerus who ruled several provinces.

Queen Vashti was Ahasuerus wife, but she disobeyed his orders and was dismissed from her position. The king was looking for a new queen and ordered that all the young and beautiful women of the provinces be recruited, including Esther. Without revealing her Jewish origin, Esther captivated King Ahasuerus with her beauty and became the Queen of Persia.

One day, Mordecai saved the king's life by setting out a plan against him. However, he did not receive any reward at that time.

Later, King Ahasuerus had trouble sleeping and asked for the books of the chronicles to be brought to him. There he read that Mordecai had saved his life in the past. He asked what reward he had received and was informed that he had not received anything. King Ahasuerus decided to honor Mordecai in gratitude and asked Prime Minister Haman what should be done to honor someone important. Haman, thinking that it was about himself, suggested that he be dressed in the king's clothes and be walked on horseback so that everyone could see him. However, to Haman's surprise, the king ordered him to do exactly that with Mordecai.

Haman, the prime minister, began to plan the destruction of the Jews due to his hatred of Mordecai, since he refused to bow down to him due to his Jewish origin.

Imagine how Haman felt about having to honor the same man he hated and for whom he had planned his death. He decided to make a gallows and sow discord between the king and Mordecai, so that the king would order his hanging.

Esther discovers Haman's plan and talks to her husband, King Ahasuerus, to save her people. It reveals its origin and exposes Haman's plans to kill the Jews and end Mordecai's life.

In this way, the king orders that Haman be hanged with the same gallows that he had prepared for Mordecai. Everything that belonged to Haman passed into the hands of Mordecai, and not only was he saved, but the death order against the Jews was also canceled.

Esther was aware that going to the king without an invitation was a risky move that could endanger her life. However, he decided to take a great risk because he understood his deep responsibility to his people. He urged the Jews to observe a fast and asked them to pray for their safety in their risky mission.

Despite having an adverse start, Esther managed to stand firm and thus save many. He focused on his purpose and the kingdom.

Approaching the king with unwavering faith and trust in God, Esther bravely revealed who he was and then begged him to save his people, the Jews, from the evil plot of Haman. Haman's evil intentions were punished when King Ahasuerus revoked the decree due to God's intervention and Esther's strong arguments.

Esther's actions show how a person's decision can have an impact even in situations of extreme danger. She taught us the value of speaking for justice and fighting for the rights of the oppressed, even if doing so endangers our personal comfort and safety.

This story also teaches us about God's invisible hand working in the background. Although God is not directly mentioned in the Book of Esther, his providential care becomes evident throughout history. The sequence of events, Esther's ascension to the throne and her influence on the king suggest divine intervention.

Today's believers can be inspired by Esther's story. This reminds us of that God always has a purpose and encourages us to have courage in the face of difficulty. It teaches us that we can change the world and that our decisions affect the lives of many people.

Esther's story is a powerful illustration of courage, faith, and disinterest. Esther's unwavering love and devotion are reflected in her choice to put her life in danger for her people. It became an instrument of God's liberation for the Jewish people through their actions. This story teaches us the importance of defending what is right, even when it endangers our own lives.

Chapter 4

Be a responsible victim

I can think back on Ester's story and conclude that sometimes we encounter unfortunate circumstances that are unanticipated, unplanned, and undeserved. But to become responsible victims, we must accept responsibility. While we cannot willfully alter the events that have happened to us, we do have the power and obligation to shape the future. We must go through a certain process to grow, heal, and break the cycle.

Our present or our future shouldn't be shaped by the past. The things we have had to endure, and face are not the fault of those around us. We develop, heal, and become able to bless others when we discover God during hardship.

Envision Esther, imprisoned in the agony of being abandoned and behaving callously and indifferently toward the person who brought her up as a daughter. Despite her possible suspicions and selfishness, she had a kind and compassionate heart. He was a willing victim.

To break the cycle and become a responsible victim, one must recognize the issue and its source. For memories to no longer cause us pain, we must also heal and learn to view them as valuable life lessons.

We also need to look at our relationships and open our eyes. This will enable us to assess whether we have recovered and surmounted the difficulties. It's time to make changes if we observe that people are moving away from us, that we are hearing critical remarks, or that our relationships feel forced and that we frequently fail in them.

It's important to find out from our loved ones what they think of us, how they feel about us, and whether we bring them acceptance, love, and serenity. Unknowingly, we can cause harm to others by not seeking healing ourselves. By growing in faith, we will be able to perceive God in every circumstance and perceive ourselves as He does. I can think back on Ester's story and conclude that sometimes we encounter unfortunate circumstances that are unanticipated, unplanned, and undeserved. But to become responsible victims, we must accept responsibility. While we cannot willfully alter the events that have happened to us, we do have the power and obligation to shape the future. We must go through a certain process to grow, heal, and break the cycle.

Our present or our future shouldn't be shaped by the past. The things we have had to endure, and face are not the fault of those around us. We develop, heal, and become able to bless others when we discover God during hardship.

Envision Esther, imprisoned in the agony of being abandoned and behaving callously and indifferently toward the person who brought her up as a daughter. Despite her possible suspicions and selfishness, she had a kind and compassionate heart. He was a willing victim.

To break the cycle and become a responsible victim, one must recognize the issue and its source. For memories to no longer cause us pain, we must also heal and learn to view them as valuable life lessons.

We also need to look at our relationships and open our eyes. This will enable us to assess whether we have recovered and surmounted the difficulties. It's time to make changes if we observe that people are moving away from us, that we are hearing critical remarks, or that our relationships feel forced and that we frequently fail in them.

It's important to find out from our loved ones what they think of us, how they feel about us, and whether we bring them acceptance, love, and serenity. Unknowingly, we can cause harm to others by not seeking healing ourselves. By growing in faith, we will be able to perceive God in every circumstance and perceive ourselves as He does. I can think back on Ester's story and conclude that sometimes we encounter unfortunate circumstances that are unanticipated, unplanned, and undeserved. But to become responsible victims, we must accept responsibility. While we cannot willfully alter the events that have happened to us, we do have the power and obligation to shape the future. We must go through a certain process to grow, heal, and break the cycle.

Our present or our future shouldn't be shaped by the past. The things we have had to endure, and face are not the fault of those around us. We develop, heal, and become able to bless others when we discover God during hardship.

Envision Esther, imprisoned in the agony of being abandoned and behaving callously and indifferently toward the person who brought her up as a daughter. Despite her possible suspicions and selfishness, she had a kind and compassionate heart. He was a willing victim.

To break the cycle and become a responsible victim, one must recognize the issue and its source. For memories to no longer cause us pain, we must also heal and learn to view them as valuable life lessons.

We also need to look at our relationships and open our eyes. This will enable us to assess whether we have recovered and surmounted the difficulties. It's time to make changes if we observe that people are moving away from us, that we are hearing critical remarks, or that our relationships feel forced and that we frequently fail in them.

It's important to find out from our loved ones what they think of us, how they feel about us, and whether we bring them acceptance, love, and serenity. Unknowingly, we can cause harm to others by not seeking healing ourselves. By growing in faith, we will be able to perceive God in every circumstance and perceive ourselves as He does.

Questions you can ask yourself.

1. Do you remember any situation that made you feel like a victim?

____

____

____

____

____

____

____

2..Who made you feel that way?

____

____

____

____

____

3. Have you been able to get over it?

____

____

____

____

____

4. How do you treat the people around you?

____

____

____

____

5. When you are under stress or price how do you react and treat others?

____

____

____

____

I If you are unable to go past these obstacles, ask God to restore your vision so that you can see Him and not the difficulties or suffering you have gone through. We cannot cling to what is around us or what was in a world where chaos and evil are on the rise and uncertainty rules.

Recall, "I'll lift my gaze to the mountains; from where will I receive assistance? The LORD, who created the earth and the heavens, is the source of my assistance." God can help you see beyond and heal your wounds. God offers you a fresh start and a fresh opportunity right where you perceive the end. God changes what appears to be death into life, and he sees an opportunity for a miracle and healing in what is presently diseased.

Isaiah 43:19 declares, "I am working on a new project that will soon be revealed. Do they not see it? I will create rivers in barren areas and roads in the desert." Thus, pray to God to help you grow in your faith.

Consider every challenge as a chance for personal development, even a chance to lend a hand to others. You can be a responsible victim in this way, allowing your past to not define who you are.

Chapter 5

The tale of the two brothers is told in Lucas. The prodigal son is the name given to one of them. One day, the younger brother shows up at his father's house asking for his portion of the inheritance. With approval, the father hands it over to her. This son, not thinking about the consequences or that he would be left with nothing one day, chooses to go far away and spends everything on sin and an unrestrained life.

One day he will experience scarcity and hunger because he will have nothing left to support himself. In the city where he is working, he gets a job feeding pigs. He becomes so hungry that all he wants to do is eat the pigs' food, but no one cares enough to feed him.

He recalls his Father's Day laborers, who have enough food, one day as he is thinking back. She makes the decision to rejoin her father. "Father, I have sinned against you and your house, I do not deserve to be called your son. Treat me like one of your day laborers," he resolves to tell his father when he returns one day. I thus made the decision to return.

His father, who is still quite a distance away, is moved when he sees him and goes to greet him. The father is the one who shows up to meet his rebellious son. Hugging him, the father gives the go-ahead for a large celebration in honor of his return. In addition, he dons a ring and his finest attire. They enjoy a magnificent feast in celebration of the fattest calf's sacrifice.

The oldest son had not been informed of what had transpired and was out in the field. He listens to music and approaches the house again, asking one of the servants what's going on. He responds, "Then your brother has returned, and your father is celebrating because his son has returned."

The elder brother chooses not to attend the celebration because he is upset. The father then goes outside and begs him to enter. However, he replies to the father, saying, "You have never even given me a child to celebrate with my friends, even though I have served you for so many years and followed all of your orders. However, when your son returns after spending all of his money on prostitutes, you throw a huge celebration for him and offer him the fattest calf as a sacrifice."

The tale of the two brothers is told in Lucas. The prodigal son is the name given to one of them. One day, the younger brother shows up at his father's house asking for his portion of the inheritance. With approval, the father hands it over to her. The dad responds: "My son, you are always with me, and all mine is yours, but we had to celebrate that your brother was dead and now he lives, he was lost, and we have found him."

The love of a father is very remarkable. The lesson of this parable is intricate and touches on many different subjects. First, it highlights the importance of personal responsibility and the consequences of our choices. Because of his irresponsible behavior and poor handling of his inheritance, the youngest son ended up penniless. This draws attention to the detrimental effects of selfishness and poor decision-making, imploring us to consider the long-term effects of the choices we make. Despite his transgressions and disobedience, the youngest son's father rushes to embrace and pardon him.

This shows God's steadfast love and his readiness to pardon anyone who sincerely asks for it. It serves as a reminder that no matter how far we have fallen or how many mistakes we have made, we can always turn to God and find forgiveness.

When his brother returns, the oldest son, who had stayed obedient and obedient to his father, becomes angry and resentful. His perspective emphasizes the peril of pursuing justice and the necessity of acting toward others with compassion and forgiveness, as God has demonstrated.

The parable also challenges our perceptions of other people. When his brother returns, the oldest son—who had stayed obedient and faithful to his father—becomes irate and resentful. From this angle, it emphasizes the perils of passing judgment on people and the necessity of acting with empathy and forgiveness toward others, as God has demonstrated.

The primary takeaway from the story of the Prodigal Son is that, despite our degree of sin or how far we may have strayed, we can always count on God's love and forgiveness if we turn back to Him in repentance. The story reminds us that God's love is undeserved and freely given. He does not need us to earn His favor once more; instead, He patiently waits for us to come back to Him so that He can heal us with His love and forgiveness.

The destructive nature of pride and self-sufficiency is also demonstrated by history. The oldest son's refusal to extend forgiveness and celebrate his brother's return serves as a lesson in the perils of harboring resentment and the value of having a gentle and modest spirit.

No matter how far we have fallen, we are always redeemable—the story of the Prodigal Son serves as a reminder of this. God's love knows no bounds, and those who seek him out in earnest can always count on his forgiveness. This narrative asks us to examine ourselves, extend forgiveness, and have faith in the restorative power of God's unfailing love.

33

Chapter 6

Love without condition

The preceding narrative provides multiple instances of forgiveness. A failed son who eventually turned around and went back home. An older brother who spills his guts, gets envious, and refuses to accept his brother's return. We witness a father who loves both of his kids equally, without bias or restriction.

The eldest brother informed his father that he had been there and had worked while the other brother had gone, indicating that he intended to pursue recognition and a benefit. Many times, we fall in love with someone in this way, or they love and admire us while we are helpful to them, but eventually their real motivations come to light, and we must part ways from them.

Even when they don't reciprocate, we shouldn't feel bad about loving and doing good because of this. We witness the younger brother who is elevated and debases himself in his heart. We must continue to have a pure, clean, and humble heart and acknowledge that we are not deserving of all the blessings God bestows upon us daily. His expressions of affection resemble those of the father in this tale. God knows everyday specifics about you and me, his children. He bestowed upon us the sun, moon, stars, sea, and wind, which cools our faces and serves as a constant reminder that we are created by God. He has bestowed upon us abilities, gifts, health, and the lovely nature that surrounds us as a sign of his great love and care.

However, much like the older brother, there are moments when we forget or hate God's eternal love in favor of the fleeting, what we want and don't have, and those who have come and gone. We can't see or appreciate that he has always been with us and that everything He has is ours because we are too preoccupied with the calf and the celebration.

The preceding narrative provides multiple instances of forgiveness. A failed son who eventually turned around and went back home. An older brother who spills his guts, gets envious, and refuses to accept his brother's return. We see a father who embodies love, sacrifice, and commitment, representing God's love for us, his children and total dedication.

This father might have accused the son of everything he had done wrong, of not appreciating his efforts as a father, of sinning and failing, and of running away from home. But when the father went to greet him after seeing him from a distance, he welcomed him with open arms. He was just relieved that his son had come back, so there was no grievance.

God loves us, his children, in this way. God is ready to embrace us and forgive all our mistakes, regardless of how many times we fall short and turn away from Him. No matter how hard we try to run away from Him, His love finds us and haunts us.

We occasionally encounter people in life who, rather than celebrating our return, wish us harm and do not want us to go back home. This older brother is one of them. For whatever reason, there are those who attempt to harm us, and as a result, we drift away from God or the church.

We must realize that the enemy we face is not physical enemies but rather spirits who have been sent to thwart God's plan for our lives. Everyone behaves in accordance with their circumstances, so try not to interpret it as a personal jab at you. Instead, it reflects the internal battles they are still fighting and have not yet won. Thus, try not to let other people's attitudes or choices influence you the extent of causing you suffering or causing you to become more distant from God.

I encourage you, like the prodigal son, to come home, cry out to God, and he will respond, if you have moved away and are sorry. God embraces you and waits for you with open arms, loving you more than anyone could ever know.

I would like you to consider these questions and take some time to respond. I'll give you some biblical verses at the end so you can prevail.

Questions you can ask yourself.

1. Have you felt that God hasn't been fair?

____

____

____

____

____

____

2.Do you feel that God is moving away from it?

____

____

____

____

____

____

3. Do you feel unworthy of God's love?

____

____

____

____

____

____

____

____

4. Do you feel dirty about your past and do you feel embarrassed to go out of God?

____

____

____

____

____

Frequently, unresolved, or untreated past wounds can act as roadblocks in our lives, leading us to distance ourselves from people and places, including churches. I want you to know and have confidence that God is with you and has never left you, regardless of the response you have written or the circumstances. He is reviving his mercy every morning because he loves you. He wants to throw a party in your honor and is waiting for you with open arms.

Chapter 7

Joseph learned a valuable lesson about rejection, and this lesson applies to anyone going through similar experiences in today's world. Joseph's brothers left him early in life, which affected José's upbringing. When he was young, his father gave him a unique multicolored tunic as a token of his important role in the family. Because of this favoritism, José's brothers would be jealous of him and would disregard his needs and emotions.

The degree of disdain Joseph felt from his own family was further highlighted when his brothers plotted to harm him. They seized the chance when their father sent him to see how his brothers were doing while they were tending to the flock. Envious and resentful, they made the decision to harm him. They took off his unique tunic and threw it into a well, intending to leave it there until it perished. Nevertheless, they sold him as a slave to a passing caravan of merchants rather than executing him.

Following his transportation to Egypt and subsequent sale to Potiphar, a pharaonic officer,

Joseph's neglectful cycle continued. Joseph demonstrated devotion and hard work in his work despite being a slave, which ultimately helped him gain his master's favor. He was consequently elevated to the position of house supervisor. But when José was falsely accused of a crime he had not committed by Potiphar's wife, his destiny abruptly changed once more. His unjust imprisonment made the abuse he had already experienced worse.

But even in prison, Joseph's spirit never wavered. He attracted the notice of the imprisoned baker and the pharaoh's cupbearer as he continued to uphold his morality and wisdom. Joseph understood his dreams correctly, and his predictions came true when the baker was put to death and the cupbearer was given back his rightful place. In the hopes that he would be released at last, José asked the cupbearer to mention it to the pharaoh; however, the cupbearer forgot, and Joseph was kept in prison even longer.

Throughout this protracted time of abandonment and hardship, Joseph never gave up hope or his belief in God. He continued to have unwavering faith in God. Before long, the pharaoh realized Joseph had a gift and summoned him to interpret a disturbing dream. God gave Joseph's interpretation, which foretold that Egypt, and the surrounding areas would experience seven years of plenty followed by seven years of famine.

Impressed by Joseph's wisdom and judgment, the pharaoh named him second in command, with overall authority over the entire nation of Egypt. Joseph's position allowed him to not only help the country prepare for the impending famine, but also to meet up with his family, who had fled to Egypt during the pandemic in search of food. In that instant, as his brothers unconsciously submitted to him, José's aspirations materialized, fully atoning for his previous history of carelessness.

We can learn a lot from this tale about unwavering loyalty, tenacity, and God's forgiveness of others. Joseph endured years of abuse, deception, and unfounded allegations, but he never gave up on God. He overcame his circumstances and accomplished his divinely appointed purpose because he upheld moral integrity and unwavering faith in God. It serves as a reminder of the importance of forgiveness. When Joseph first met his brothers, he showed them genuine love and forgiveness rather than taking revenge or harboring resentment. This act of forgiveness not only healed his family's division but also provided a potent example of God's kindness and grace in our own lives.

Even in the worst of times, Joseph never wavered in his resistance or faith. He never wavered in his love for God or in his conviction that there was more to life, even in the face of suffering. This unwavering faith served as a ray of hope for him the entire way, enabling him to overcome his circumstances and, in the end, alter the course of history.

Joseph's vision helps us comprehend how rejection affects individuals. To begin with, inattention can cause jealousy, animosity, and discord in families. It highlights how important it is to treat every family member equally, lovingly, and without favoritism—a behavior that can plant the seeds of strife.

This gives us insight into the value of forgiveness and our capacity to move past abandonment. After experiencing his own blood being rejected, Joseph extended forgiveness to his brothers when they later sought his assistance. Not only did his forgiveness mend their relationship, but it also showed how healing and transformational forgiveness can be.

This acts as a reminder that an individual's worth, and future are not influenced by the abandonment they have encountered. Despite being abandoned and mistreated, José never wavered in his dedication and focus on his objectives. With perseverance, hard work, and faith in God, he was able to overcome slavery and rise to become a powerful and important leader in Egypt.

Joseph's ascent to fame, his talent for interpreting dreams, and his contribution to averting famine in Egypt are proof that rejection does not have the final say. This story offers redemption, resistance, and hope to those who have been overlooked or forgotten.

The biblical story of Joseph teaches us valuable lessons about abandonment and its impact on individuals. He stresses how important it is to treat every member of the family with love and equality and to refrain from showing favoritism, which can breed jealousy and resentment. It is a living example of the ability to change oneself and the transforming force of forgiveness. Joseph's story serves as an inspiration to those who have been neglected, as it serves as a reminder that his worth and destiny are predicated on his own faith, perseverance, and capacity to believe in a higher purpose beyond the actions of others.

Chapter 8

Recognizing that rejection isn't always about us will help us manage it. People occasionally encounter unfamiliar circumstances and instinctively put up a barrier. Sometimes they just recall someone who has wronged us, causing all our bad feelings to surface. Rejection by a partner can damage our self-esteem and cause us to doubt who we are.

It's critical to realize that we bear no responsibility for the things that other people do to us. Everybody donates in proportion to their means. When a leader is rejected, we may start to doubt ourselves and our potential; it may even have an impact on our faith.

Our fear of being abandoned can arise from being rejected by our parents or a close relative. Since we feel unworthy of their love and acceptance, we even attempt to buy or gain their love and acceptance by doing things that we think show how valuable we are.

This makes us fearful of giving up or clinging to others for fear that they will one day leave us, and we will experience the same emotions as when our parents did, making us feel unworthy of their love or companionship. The way we embrace or reject God's love in our lives reflects this.

Rejection of any kind can make us feel guilty or accountable for everything that happens to us if we are unable to confront or overcome it. It's critical to realize that it is unrelated to us. People who are willing to love, support, and care for you shouldn't be turned away. Above all, remember that you are loved and valued by your heavenly Father, and don't let anyone break your heart.

It might help to keep in mind that Jesus was rejected even though he didn't deserve it to overcome rejection. We are fighting against spirits and demons that are trying to turn us away from God, make us feel unworthy of his love, grace, and salvation, and cause us to see ourselves differently than He does.

Never forget that you are incredibly valuable, loved, accepted, and forgiven. Put the people who rejected you behind you and pray for them to face their inner struggles rather than dwelling on them. Consider God's immense and boundless love.

Any attitude of abandonment and rejection must be let go of. Stop the cycle. Always demonstrate God's love by accepting and loving everyone.

Questions you can ask yourself.

1. Will you be enough?

____

____

____

____

____

____

____

____

2. Will it be that I am active?

____

____

____

____

____

I want you to write a list of the people or things that have hurt you, as well as a list of the people who love you. Next, list your advantages and disadvantages. Write what God has to say about you in the end.

____
____
____
____
____
____
____
____
____
____
____
____
____
____

After that, forgive them and offer prayers for them. Additionally, pray to God for the ability to value and love the people who have supported and loved you. Lastly, ask God to help you see yourself from his perspective. The only way we can love properly is via God's love.

You can accept God's love for you and his sacrifice of saving you and giving you eternal life by fully loving yourself. Recall that 1 John 3:1-2 states that we are loved and now God's children. Regardless of what people think or say, God and who He says we are the only ones who can truly define who we are.

Chapter 9

One of the most well-known figures in the biblical book of Esther is Mordecai, who represents God's timely intervention in his people's lives. His narrative emphasizes the importance of tenacity, bravery, and trust in divine providence, particularly during trying times.

A Jew from the tribe of Benjamin named Mordecai was one of the captives in the Persian Empire during the reign of Ahasuerus. Even in captivity, Mordecai never shied away from his heritage or identity. She raised her cousin Esther as if she were her own daughter after her parents passed away, acting as a father figure for the young woman.

The central theme of Mordecai's narrative is his unwavering fidelity to God. He faced off against Haman, a strong and arrogant king official who harbored hatred for both Mordecai and all Jews in general. Aman started preparing the destruction of every Jew in the kingdom in retaliation for this act of rebellion. As soon as Mordecai realized his people were in grave danger, he acted quickly and called Esther, pleading with her to use her authority as queen to protect her people.

This is the moment when God's amazing intervention becomes apparent. Initially, Esther was terrified to go to the king by herself because she might end up dead if she did. But Mordecai reminded her quite forcefully that maybe she had been made queen "for a time like this." This expression captures the idea that God works through particular people at times to accomplish his goals.

Encouraged by Mordecai's words and driven by her love for her people, Esther found the courage to approach the king. Through a meticulously orchestrated series of events, God miraculously changed Aman's circumstances. Aman was made to answer for his misdeeds after the plot to exterminate the Jews was uncovered.

The story of Mordecai teaches us something important about when God intervenes. God may appear silent or not answer right away when faced with challenges, but his plans are quietly being carried out in the background. Mordecai's unshakable faith in God's timing makes him an inspiration to all of us. He understood that God's plan for Esther's coronation ultimately aimed to spare his people from certain death.

In our own lives, we may encounter situations that make us feel as though God has forgotten us, abandoned us, or both. We might ask ourselves why it seems like we are up against insurmountable challenges and that no one is answering our prayers. However, the Mordecai story serves as a reminder that everything occurs precisely as God desires. He may not always have the same plans as us, but he always has the final say.

We must trust in God's providence and be obedient even in the direst circumstances. Just as Mordecai God's unwavering faith ultimately resulted in his people's salvation, so too can our faith in God's timing work wonders in our own lives.

The Mordecai story also demonstrates the community's resilience and togetherness in the face of adversity. Mordecai's call to Esther was not merely a private entreaty; rather, the Jewish people needed to come together and work toward God's liberation as a collective. His prayers and deeds together demonstrated his faith in God and his will to oppose the forces of evil.

The narrative of Mordecai imparts to us the crucial lesson of trusting in God's providence and timing. The same way that he shaped Mordecai's life to keep the Jewish people from being destroyed, he is intimately involved in our lives. We know that God will provide for us at the perfect time, so when things get tough, we must stay obedient, brave, and one.

Chapter 10

God arrives on time

We frequently question why horrible things occur to decent people and good things to bad people. We occasionally wonder about God's justice and why people who commit evil seem to live better lives or to benefit from more advantages.

First, despite being sinless and the only Son of God, Jesus endured rejection, beatings, betrayals, and a lack of faith from many. Jesus took the punishment he did because he loved us, even though he didn't deserve it. Jesus did, however, once feel abandoned and cried out to the Father, "Why have you abandoned me?" during his humanity. He also uttered the desperate words, "If it's possible, take this cup away from me, but let your will be done."

Here, we observe how nice people appear to suffer bad things without taking pleasure in it. But we must have complete faith that God will provide for us and that everything will work out for the best.

In Esther's narrative, we meet Mordecai, her uncle, who adopted her as a daughter and brought her up as though she were his own following her father's passing. It is possible to describe Mordecai as a man of great heart, noble, good feelings, responsibility, and fear of God. However, Aman, a high ranking official of King Ahasuerus, appears in the story as it is told in the book of Esther. He was a self-assured and aspirational man who wanted men to bow down to him and worship him.

Because Mordecai was a Jew and would not bow down before Ahasuerus, Ahasuerus became desirous of taking his own life. Ahasuerus commanded that all Jews be killed to eradicate Mordecai as well. When he saw that many Jews were being killed, Mordecai became upset about the injustice and went into mourning. He did not, however, ever bow down before Ahasuerus; instead, he was always afraid of God and was treated with respect.

It might appear unjust, doesn't it? And I would have questioned the location of the just God who permits such suffering.

In the narrative, we witness how Mordecai one day saves the king's life, but the king does not give him credit right away. But afterwards, the king recalls this and chooses to pay tribute to Mordecai. Knowing the circumstances, Queen Esther makes the decision to step in. At last, God executes justice justly, and Mordecai receives his reward—becoming the second in command.

We can learn from this story that God is just and that everything has its proper place and time. Even though it may seem like things aren't going our way at times, we must remain silent and have faith in God. Without wavering in our faith, we must continue to be faithful to Him and ask for mercy.

I would like you to consider this tale and consider God's mercy, which is extended to both us and those who have wronged us. Regardless of one's circumstances, everyone shed the blood of Christ. We must therefore forgive and have faith in God. He defends our position while we behave properly.

If something goes wrong or doesn't work out the way you planned, don't give up. It can seem at times like God is unresponsive to our prayers or absent when we most need him. But even as He silently shapes us through our trials, He never leaves our side. God is perfect, and he has the perfect time. When we act appropriately, we will emerge from the tests changed.

God never fails to work for our good, even when it isn't apparent to us. Therefore, we must exercise patience and trust that God will guide us in the right direction and manifest Himself on schedule. Trust that He is working in your life and get ready to come out of the test stronger and with new insights.

Questions you can ask yourself.

1. Why do we sometimes ask ourselves why bad things happen to the good gentle and bad people do well?

____

____

____

____

____

____

____

____

____

2.How can we trust that, despite the injustices, God will always come to our aid and work for our good?

____

____

____

____

3. What does the story of Mordecai teach us in relation to God's justice and how we can persevere in faith despite making it difficult?

____

____

____

____

____

4. How can we avoid falling into temptation and making bad decisions according to the text?

____

____

____

____

5. What is the importance of seeking God's direction before making decisions and opening our hearts to people?t

____

____

____

I invite you to reflect on the history you have read before and meditate on God's mercy, which is available both to you and to those who have hurt you and done you wrong. The blood of Christ was shed by every human being, regardless of their condition. Therefore, forgive and trust in God. Fight for what is right while maintaining your faith.

If something goes wrong or doesn't work out the way you planned, don't give up. It can appear at times that God is unresponsive to our prayers or that he disappears just when we most need him. He can keep quiet while our experiences shape who we are. God is perfect, and he has the perfect time. You won't be the same after the test if you don't behave appropriately. Even when we cannot see him or understand him, he always works in our best interests. Because of this, we must wait patiently and with faith, trusting that God will show up on schedule and lead us in the correct direction.

Chapter 11

Women subject to bleeding

The account of a woman who endured a disease—more precisely, a blood flow—for twelve years of her life is found in Mark 5:25–34. He spent all his money on medical care and still didn't find relief. But one day, he learned of Jesus' capacity to heal the ill. He made the decision to come to Him in need of assistance, full of hope and faith.

Because of the throng that surrounded Jesus, the woman came up behind him and touched the hem of her mantle, thinking that she would be healed simply by touching him. And so it came to pass that he sensed his ailment had vanished right away.

Jesus turned to face the crowd and questioned who had touched him after recognizing the power that had come from Him. While the disciples gestured toward the dense throng, Jesus turned to face whoever had touched him. The woman knelt before Him and told him the whole truth, terrified but aware of what had transpired within.

In response, Jesus addressed her as "daughter" and told her that she had been saved by her faith. He wished her well after her suffering and urged her to leave in peace.

The woman had to face several challenges before she could come to know Jesus, including rejection from others, shame over her perceived impurity, and the necessity of defying social norms to seek treatment.

It is astounding to see that in addition to her faith, the woman possessed a strong will and a profound need that only she could comprehend. This gave her the motivation to act and get past every barrier in her path. He took the action that would permanently alter his life. Faith without deeds is dead.

This story reminds us how important it is to keep going after the healing and well-being we so desperately need, despite the hurdles and judgments of others. It inspires us to have a proactive faith and be prepared to act to receive the blessing that is right at our fingertips.

Chapter 12

Without movement there is no fulfillment

I've told this story before, and it holds a lot of significance for me. I was bleeding, too, but it was internal bleeding, like the sick woman. Since I was a young child, years of suffering have defined my life. He bore numerous burdens that were clearly visible and grew heavier over time, including hurt, hatred, and guilt. My character and personality were defiant, and I was incapable of truly loving someone. I tried everything the world had to offer and lived an empty life, but nothing could make me better.

He knew Jesus, having grown up in the church, but not fully. Up until the day I sought a miracle, just like that woman. I came to God full of uncertainties, fears, and weaknesses, and he healed my heart, set me free from vices, and showed me how to love. I discovered how to love and forgive people who had let me down and hurt me. My life has completely changed since that day. Perhaps, like me, you have spent years trying to break free from the hurt, the unforgiveness, and the memories that caused you pain. Perhaps you've had enough of attempting everything on your own and finding that nothing works for you.

Perhaps you've been going through trying times for years and you're hoping for a miracle—a response from God. Sometimes, to fill a void that only God can, we search for answers in things that seem right in our eyes, even in vices.

She claims to have heard of Jesus in verse 21 and came up behind him, declaring, "If I only touch the edge of her mantle, I will be healed." Her blood flow stopped, and she was healed the instant she touched him.

Jesus listens to you when you call on Him and ask for a miracle or salvation. She had to accept that she was sick and that there was nothing she could do to improve herself before she could experience her miracle. She had faith that she would have faith and choose to seek Jesus' miracle after hearing from him.

She was indifferent to the opinions of others, criticism, jeers, or rejection. He decided to accept salvation and healing despite all obstacles. Her decision changed her life, and I'm impressed by how she overcame all of that.

Questions you can ask yourself.

1. Write down those things that in life have prevented you from reaching fulfillment, holiness, liberation?

____

____

____

____

2. What have you done to change your condition or heal those internal wounds?

____

____

____

____

3. Do you know Jesus, do you just talk about him?

____

____

____

____

Please accept my invitation to let God heal every aspect of your life by opening your heart. The Bible says that we only need as much faith as a mustard seed, so you don't need to have a lot of it.

In Jairo's case, his daughter was ill, so he needed a miracle. While Jesus was on his way home, he asked for assistance. During the crowd, a woman who was bleeding profusely approached Jesus and touched the edge of his mantle, instantly becoming healed. Jesus was informed of the girl's passing by messengers who had arrived in the interim. "Jairo, your daughter is not dead, she's just asleep," Jesus said in response.

Certain things must die in us for the new of God to arise in us during our lifetime. Among the many things that keep us from progressing and becoming free are fear, hatred, criticism, accusations, what they will say, a lack of forgiveness, and conformity. We must let these things die. When Jesus went to a person's home, he did not put up any obstacles or tell the woman to "wait for her to be busy." Often, we end up being the biggest hindrance to ourselves to accomplish the miracle we require. Jesus is always ready to hear us out, to accept us, to heal and purify us, and to extend to us the offer of salvation and everlasting life. Thus, don't hesitate any longer and approach Him.

There is only one who can heal you completely and love you above all things. Jesus is waiting for you with open arms.

Chapter 13

In the book of Judges 13-16 we can find the story of Samson. He was an Israelite judge and leader who possessed a supernatural force due to a promise that an angel said to his mother when it appeared to him one day. 3 The angel of the LORD appeared to this woman, and said to her, "Behold, you are barren, and have never had children; but you shall conceive and give birth to a son. 4 Now, therefore, drink not wine, nor cider, nor eat an unclean thing.5 For behold, you shall conceive and bear a son; and a knife will not pass over his head, for the child will be a Nazarene to God from his birth, and he will begin to save Israel by the hand of the Philistines.6 And the woman came and told it to her husband, saying, A man of God came to me, whose appearance was like The appearance of an angel of God, fearful in a great way; and I did not ask him from where or who he was, nor did he say his name to me. 7 and he said to me: Behold, you will conceive, and you shall give birth to a son; therefore, now drink not drink wine, or cider, or eat unclean things, for this child will be a

Nazarene to God from his birth to the day of his death.

Samson was born and raised; from his youth he demonstrated great physical strength and performed amazing feats. However, he was also known for his weakness towards the Philistine women, who were enemies of Israel. Samson is known for his superhuman strength and his unbreakable self-confidence. However, the story of Samson also teaches us the importance of not being fooled by the appearances and the true source of our strength. Despite his divine call, Samson often let himself be carried away by his desires and approached temptation.

One of Samson's most notable weaknesses was his attraction to Philistine women. Although God had warned him about the dangers of these relationships, Samson insisted on marrying a Philistine woman named Dalila. The story of Samson and Delilah is famous since Dalilah betrayed Samson by discovering the source of his strength by cutting his hair. The story of Samson and Dalilah teaches us an important lesson about confidence in appearances at first sight, Delilah seemed to have good feelings towards Samson, but his purpose was to betray him and weaken him. His beauty and charm disguised his true nature. Samson, unfortunately, fell into the trap of.believing in the apparent goodness of someone who did not deserve his trust. This lesson invites us to reflect on our own lives and the relationships we forge.

Often, we let ourselves be carried away by external appearances and trust those who seem friendly and benevolent. However, as the story of Samson teaches us, beauty and charm do not guarantee loyalty and kindness. Instead of blindly relying on appearances, we must look beyond the surface and evaluate people's actions and motives. This does not mean that we should distrust everyone, but that we must be cautious and not easily get carried away by deceptive appearances.

We must truly get to know people before we give them our trust. Likewise, as followers of God, it is important to remember that our true strength comes from Him and not from our physical appearance or abilities. Be careful who we meet with. Samson's story shows us that even the strongest person can be overthrown when he puts his trust in earthly things instead of God. Samson lost his strength when he lost his connection to the divine purpose.

Chapter 14

Listen to the voice of God and obey

As Samson we often ignore the voice of God and the warnings that He gives us so that we do not fall into temptation and do not make bad decisions. God is interested in our well-being in every area of our lives.

Sometimes the problem is that we open our hearts to the wrong people and end up suffering consequences and sometimes we get hurt, but it is easier for us to blame God than to assume our responsibility in that many times we do not obey God or keep his word.

Samson opened his heart to the wrong person, and this led him to be betrayed. Even so, God fulfilled his purpose in him. The problem is not that we trust people, the problem is that we do not seek God's direction. To avoid this, the answer is not to become cold and indifferent to the Others.

Rather, we must seek God's direction before making decisions and opening our hearts. Not every person who goes your way is to stay and you should not open your heart to everyone and give your trust. One of the biggest problems of the human being is that we seek to fill empty spaces and satisfy our life by surrounding ourselves with people, waiting for approval from man, or sometimes we look for him in vices and even material things taking from God the place that only He deserves.

We were created to glorify God and live for Him, that's why nothing outside of Him can satisfy or fill us. No matter how good a heart we have, we are all imperfect and with a sinful nature that's why people fail, but God remains faithful Sometimes we make more effort to please people than to live to please God who is the only one who can love you and take care of you as you need it, his love has no limits or conditions. There is nothing we can do to deserve his love or for him to stop loving us.

God loves even the sinner, but he hates sin. He is willing to fill your life, guide your steps and fulfill his purpose in you.

Questions you can ask yourself.

1.What is the importance of seeking God's direction before making decisions and opening our hearts to people?

____

____

____

____

____

____

2.What does this chapter teach us about God's unconditional love and his willingness to fill our lives and fulfill his proposal in us?

____

____

____

____

____

We should not trust our emotions or feelings if they are not first proven and approved by God. Jeremiah 17:9-10 Deceptive is the heart more than all things and perverse Who will know it? I, the Lord, who scrutinize the mind and test the heart, to give to each one according to his way according to the fruit of his works. Be careful who you trust. Fix your gaze on Jesus and always look for his direction. Psalms 147:3 God heals those who have broken hearts. Bandage their wounds.

Chapter 15

Self-examining ourselves is not an easy job, because for humanity from creation, from Adam and Eve it is easier to look for culprits to justify our bad actions and wrong decisions. Justifying our bad behaviors only enclose us and tie us to a past or contrary feelings that give us a great weight on us and inadvertently affect those around us (generational curses).

Imagine that every situation you have faced in life in a potato, and you have carried them with you inside a sack during your life. Each of them is decomposing more and more, it is rotting and when you enter a good one it will be damaged along with the others. The state of decomposition produces a very unpleasant smell. Imagine carrying this bag for months or years, everyone around you will notice the bad smell. Now compare this to situations in your life.

Every time something negative or unpleasant happens to you and you accumulate it little by little, contrary feelings and attitudes grow that affect both you and others. Over time it will be so much resentment or distrust that you will not be able to enjoy good people and give them the best of you because you carry a bag of rotten potatoes and each potato in good condition is swindled and damaged by the others (that is, you can't see the beauty of life or enjoy the love of God in its entirety because bad experiences, unhealed wounds do not allow you.

Without realizing it, we give for less the sacrifice of Jesus on the cross for love of you and me even without deserving it. Jesus received the worst punishment; I took your guilt and mine and gave us the greatest sign of forgiveness and love. Jesus forgives everyone who betrays him, denied him, hurts him, made fun of him, and forgives our offenses every day. Jesus being perfect and just, without deserving it, carried our guilt and gave us forgiveness and eternal life. So why is it difficult for us to forgive and love? We must understand that everyone gives what they have according to their ability, therefore, it should not reflect us, but that we must understand that we all fight and day by day we face situations that mark us for better or for worse as we decide. Your attitude to each situation should reveal to yourself who you are if you have healed and what areas you must still surrender to God in prayer. This is a process that involves time, willpower, disposition, and discipline.

Opening your heart will sometimes hurt you because you will have to come face to face with that or with those who grieved and hurt you, but it is the best we can do and only dare God and his Holy Spirit can we achieve it. *Cry out to me and I will answer you.

Ask God in prayer to show you every sin in your life that is hidden and lack of forgiveness. You can make a list according to God to remind you of even those times when you failed yourself and then pray and release forgiveness. Examine my heart I must break negative habits, overcome the Criticism, the rejection, the Pointing. Over everything kept keep your heart Clean your heart and renew your mind Proverbs 28:13 He who covers his sins will not prosper, but he who confesses and abandons them will achieve mercy.

Blessed is the man who always fears God, but he who hardens his heart will fall into evil. It is necessary to recognize, identify and confess in prayer to be free and heal. Father, we come in front of you in the same feeling! We call on you to take care of me and everything you read in this book. I know that you will glorify yourself in everything we do for you.

Teach us to open our heart and mind in what you have prepared for us. Be your guide of our steps and our plans. Examine our heart and start what prevents us from growing on your way. It covers every family, my house, and those around me. We ask you for all this in the name of Jesus. Amen!

OPEN YOUR HEART

OPEN YOUR HEART

OPEN YOUR HEART